I See You, I S

A beautiful and poignant collection of poems gathered from those who all have a personal connection with the care of others.

Illustrated by Annabelle Hoyle
Edited and cover design by Jane Eaglesome

Copyright©Pandon Ltd 2023
All rights reserved

WARNING Copyright of this publication in its design and format is owned by Pandon Ltd. To photocopy or reproduce by any method without prior permission from Pandon Ltd is prohibited.
Copyright of individual illustrations is owned by Annabelle Hoyle and Samantha Kilburn.
Copyright of the individual poems is owned by each author as credited.

Preface

I SEE YOU is a community social fund that aims to help care for adults who have entered the care system without financial backing, the absence of family or friends for help or support and reliant totally on local authority funding.

People in this situation receive funding that covers the care/nursing home fees only and it is very difficult for them to access further funds for personal items such as clothes, shoes, haircuts, toiletries etc. It can also prove a very lengthy process obtaining these funds and sadly, time, is not something many of these people have remaining.

Being alone at such a vulnerable time of life is heartbreaking and then to find themselves unable to have the financial means to buy basic clothing, keep hair tidy, buy a snug pair of slippers or shoes is so desperately sad.

Brunelcare is a charity in itself but here at Glastonbury Care Home we have launched the I See You Fund specifically to help vulnerable people who reside in care.

Each and every care home that looks after local authority funded residents will have people that find themselves in this situation at one time or another. Many will have experienced just how difficult it is to access additional funding for personal needs. Care staff will often donate or buy the items they need from their own wages.

Our aim is for people in care homes who do not have the financial means to buy the basics of life to know that we see you, you exist and we will help you.

Every poem in this book has been written by someone who has had personal experience of caring for others whether it be nursing, care or relatives. These poems have all been written from the heart and donated to this book for the purpose of raising awareness and raising important funds to improve lives.

Thank you to everyone who has contributed and a special thank you to Annabelle Hoyle whose beautiful illustrations bring the poems to life.

Annabelle Hoyle

Having studied education at university Annabelle works as a nursery educator. When not at work Annabelle finds solace and joy by capturing moments through a lens, photographing as much as possible wherever she may be. Annabelle also follows lots of different sports including F1, netball and football.

Having drawn all her life mainly as a therapeutic outlet to unwind and express creativity, this is Annabelle's first opportunity to have sketches published and seen by people outside of the family

Inspiration for these drawings has come from being a devoted mummy of a young son who is autistic, seeking out nature to help regulate himself, feeling his sense of calm from being outside and the memories shared exploring the Somerset countryside together.

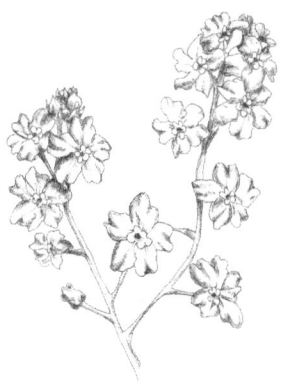

Contents

- **Pearl** - Amelia Davis
- **Tomorrow** - Joan Murphy
- **The Wildness of Things** - Emily Eaglesome
- **Dementia** - Briony Hurd
- **Mirror Image** - Grace Harvey
- **Words of Wisdom** - Samantha Hurd
- **Just Believe** - Joan Murphy
- **Nursery Rhymes With A Twist** - Grace Harvey
- **Life (As We Know It)** - Sandra Pike
- **Dedicated To My Grandchildren** - Grace Harvey
- **The Tale of Mr Nibbles** - Nanny Murphy
- **Remember When Mum** - Jo Taylor
- **Momento Mori** - Emily Eaglesome
- **Lyrics From A Love Song** - Paul Denegri
- **When We Nurse We Care** - Nina
- **Our Home** - Staff & Residents of The Cyder Barn
- **The Snowflake** - Donald Denegri
- **I'm Telling Your Father** - Jo Taylor

- **The Brook** - Joan Murphy
- **Let's Get Rocked** - Jon Bon Jovi's Boots
- **Overboard** - Simon Denegri
- **Autumn Wind** - Samual Gwilliam
- **Rainbow Scarves** - Samantha Kilburn
- **Under the Old Willow Tree** - Samantha Kilburn
- **My Day** - Shirley
- **I No Longer Dare To Care** - Samantha Kilburn
- **I'm Tired** - Harriet Lewis
- **New Admission** - William Muchochomi
- **Remembering You** - Simon Denegri
- **Dawn** - Donald Denegri
- **Thanks From A Student Nurse** - Amelia Davis
- **Alone In Rio** - Simon Denegri
- **The Devil** - Joan Murphy
- **Remember Me** - Donald Denegri

Pearl

Hold my hand for a little while and then we can walk
Across golden sand barefoot and then we can talk
I close my eyes and see the sun dance upon the deep blue sea
Hold my hand a little while just you and me.
Hold my hand a little while and through green fields
Where wildlife live and golden wheat yields.
Through green woods where the sunlight sparkles through the trees
The smell of grass, the buzzing of the bees.
I close my eyes I am tired, hold my hand a little while
So I can drift to the world I loved and made me smile.

By Amelia Davis RMN
Nurse at GCH

Tomorrow

If life was full of sunshine
With never any rain
And all our days be full of joy
With never any pain
And if there was no sorrow
Or reason for our tears
What would we have to hope for
How would we spend our years?
For when the rain has ended
We look forward to the sun
And when our pain has ended
Our joy and hope be one
And when our eyes once more are dry
And hope replaces sorrow
We'll forget what happened yesterday
And look forward to Tomorrow.

Joan Murphy

The Wildness of Things

The Wildness of Things

You can Never not see the wildness of things.
In sweet spells cast by the songbird
When life roars into bewitching Spring
and Never can you see the shy white deadnettle
With its pearl-budded plimsoles adorned
And think not of sleepy faeries sipping tea from acorn kettles
Nor munching mushrooms as they yawn
You can Never not see the magic of a star-grazed sky
Nor Never not feel it when a love's gaze greets your eye
Nor do you not dream for Summer's soft rain
to kiss your gentle flesh and leave pixie dust stains
and Never not in decay is enchantment too
as you rot into me and I rot into you
and how could I Ever not feel this magical
to know I will enmesh with the wildness of things.
For-ever and for-all.

**Emily Eaglesome
Daughter of GCH Employee**

Dementia

I had to move to a new home as I was feeling ill
I had to leave my little flat behind
And all the memories it had.
I had to start a new adventure in a world I didn't know
Because dementia had a hold of me and my mind was not my own.

I met some lovely friends we chatted and we knitted
But deep down in mind there was stuff I knew going missing.
My Grandchildren were filtering out of my mind,
But seeing photos and hearing tales brightened my day.

I then became so poorly I had to move again,
The memories I had made had gone once more.
I didn't know my name, my age or where I was,
I didn't know my family which was hard for me you know.

My body was here but my mind was gone
I wasn't myself but people still come.
I can't hold conversations but I know they're there,
Hearing their voices and knowing they cared.

I am now up in heaven and my mind is free,
The memories I had came flooding back to me.
I look down on my family and send them all my love,
I wish I could have done that before I went above.

Briony Hurd
In memory of Mum in Law

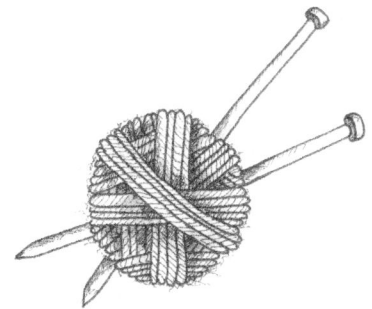

Mirror Image

When I look in the mirror what do I see?
A person who looks older -- older than me.
Glasses perched on the end of her nose,
To help her see clearly -- I suppose.
Lines on her face and a chin that is double,
Heaven forbid!! I think I see stubble,
Hair now going grey, boobs that do sag,
Hips that much wider and eyes that have bags,
Where have I gone? What's happened to me?
Perhaps it's because I'm now seventy three.
So ladies if we want to look like young ravers,
Just let's take off our glasses and stay away from Spec Savers.

Grace Harvey
Ex Brunelcare Employee

Mirror Image

Words of Wisdom

Old people,
with their words of wisdom,
are treasure troves of life's lessons.
We listen to their stories,
cherish their presence,
and learn from their resilience.
For in their wrinkled smiles,
we find the essence of humanity,
and the legacy of a life well-lived.

Their laughter, like gentle echoes,
fills the room with warmth,
reminding us of the joy
that comes from simple pleasures.
They have loved and lost,
worked and struggled,
and now, in their twilight years,
they seek solace and peace.

Samantha Hurd

Just Believe

Just believe there's somewhere else
Where we will meet again
A place of love and happiness
All free from sin and pain
A land where we'll meet loved ones
And friends who passed before
All waiting there to greet us
How could we ask for more
So just go on believing
That dreams sometimes come true
It will help you through your sorrow
And your life much easier too

Joan Murphy - written for Sylvia on the passing of her husband

Nursery Rhymes With A Twist

Little Miss Muffet sat on a tuffet eating her curds and whey,
When along came Tommy Tucker singing for his supper,
Cos poor lad he hadn't eaten all day.
Then he saw Jack Horner sat in a corner eating a great plum pie,
and as Tommy grabbed for a slice along came three blind mice
And whisked the whole lot away.
The Farmer's wife she took off with a knife,
She were determined to cut off their tails.
But they climbed up the clock, cos hey, dickory dock,
They were afraid for their bits- they were males.
Then Bo Beep came by she'd lost her sheep,
She asked Blue Boy to find them.
So he blew his horn from late night until morn, till Hey diddle diddle,
He found the cat and the fiddle and the sheep but they'd all been shorn,
Now Jack and Jill went up the hill never mind the pail of water,
What Jack had in mind for Jill well he didn't really ought to !!!
Ba Ba black sheep ran amok scattering the ewes in Bo Peep's flock,
Humpty Dumpty fell off the wall while playing with the King's men,
They were having a ball!
Cock Robin was killed with a bow and arrow,
Shot through the head by a wayward sparrow,
Mary Mary quite contrary was tending her garden fair,
When Wee Willy Winky streaked through the town giving his bits an air.
So the Owl and the Pussy Cat took him to sea,
In their beautiful pea green boat,
And as far as I am aware,
He's still out there wrapped up in a five pound note.

Grace Harvey
Ex Brunelcare Employee

Life (as we know it)

Masks, temperatures, lateral flow.
These are the things that we have
come to know.
Visitors and family coming in
The joy on the faces of people within.
Meeting in the garden was good to
see, celebrating our Queens
Platinum Jubilee
Quizzes, painting and much much more,
the people who live here have
come to adore.
Staff go about their daily tasks
A request to them is not too much to ask.
Longing for the day the masks will
come off, for our caring smile is
what they've dreamed of.

Sandra Pike
Retired Homemaker GCH

Dedicated to my Grandchildren

A little hand slips into mine, two eyes look up at me,
And I am overwhelmed with love, and happy as can be.
For I am now a Nanny and privileged to share,
In lots of small adventures, or just to stop and stare,
At the wonder of a spider's web and the chrysalis we found,
The busy little ants as they scurry underground,
At the little face raised up to me and the question on those lips,
Like 'Nan where does the cuckoo go and who eats all the hips?"
We hear the noisy chattering and scolding as we near,
And the wonder on that little face when a squirrel did appear.
We watch the buzzard circle and hear the pheasant call,
And hunt for empty snail shells hidden in the wall.
We creep up on the rabbits, that are lying in the sun.
My grandchild smiles happily, " Oh Nan we're having fun".

Yes I am truly privileged, I have something more than gold.
I have grandchildren to love and small hands that I can hold.

Grace Harvey
Ex Brunelcare Employee

The Tale of Mr Nibbles

This is the tale of Nibbles the rabbit.
Who had the most annoying habit
And although he liked the grass that grows
He also liked to eat one's toes
And poor old Granny in her chair
Was fast asleep and unaware
That Nibbles was sizing up her feet
He wanted something good to eat
So starting with the smallest digit
He chewed away, Nan didn't fidget
She never felt the slightest pain
So Nibs just carried on again
He nibbled both her wrinkled feet
And thought how good they were to eat
He chewed each leg up to her knees
But the hairy bits just made him sneeze
Poor Gran woke up with such a start
She screamed out loud and clutched her heart

"Alas!" she cried " Where are my feet!"
Then tried to get up from her seat
She fell right down upon her bottom
And said to Nibs "You're really rotten!"
" Fancy eating both my legs!"
"I'll have to buy some wooden pegs
So don't sit there Nibs looking smug
I'll show you that I'm not a mug...
Now that you are not so thin...
I'm going to eat you for my din!"

Nanny Murphy
Nan of deputy manager GCH Thomas Knauer

Mr Nibbles

Remember When Mum?

I'm sitting by the window
I'm looking for you Mum but you never come
I'm living in a care home you see Mum?
I've something called dementia you see?
I want to jump in puddles remember Mum?
Oh how we laughed my brothers, sisters and me
Playing cowboys and Indians, hop-scotch, marbles and jacks.
And all for free, it didn't cost a penny did it Mum?
Oh how we laughed Mum, climbing trees, scraping knees,
jumping ditches.
My brothers, sisters and me.

Oh how I want to see you Mum
And to just sit on your knee.
Oh here's the lovely carer with my cup of tea.
She's lovely Mum, she has a smile all the time.
Just like you Mum, she sees me Mum
Oh how I wish I could see you
How I long to sit on your knee.

Jo Taylor, Housekeeper GCH

Remember when Mum

Memento Mori

Bereaved streetlights blink, teary-eyed,
as blinds of Dusk draw down, to mourn,
a murder of crows shriek
elegies of fraticide
and grieving clouds wander,
forlorn.

Blood ablaze seeps through cracks
in heaven's highest floor,
draining both the sun
and the soft, small star of my body;
although it has done before,
it still darkens ever I,
now the night has killed the day
and the dark fills the sky.

But the Moon whispers wild lullabies
to the full, summer breeze
and leaves light kisses on my
heavy-lidded eyes,
there is no need for your sleepy sorrow;
as sure as Spring is to Winter, murmurs she–
the Sun burns brighter
Tomorrow–

Emily Eaglesome, Daughter of GCH employee

Lyrics from a love song

As we struggle with life's gradients
Our love carries us higher
Our steps grow stronger, firmer
We pull each other hand in hand
Taking turns to lead the other

When we reach the summit
We stand together
On the brink of all we hoped
Looking out on the world
On the edge of our dreams

As we look down on the world
We see the path we've travelled
Valleys, quicksands, rough places, plains
These will be our past
Now it will be our love that reigns

But at this brow of life
If still shadows darken and trees wither
Our view obscured, the rivers dry
What brought us to the summit
Will carry you and I again

The sun may not shine or the world delight
But our love is strong, deeper for our climb
Because our love was never cruel or hard
Only soft and warm, smooth, accepting
robust, strong, closely intimate

As we close the door leave the world outside
The two of us alone
It's then I really feel how beautiful you are
How love is meant to go
Your touch is all I need to know.

As we lose ourselves to even time itself
I don't want to let you go
For this is our paradise
And it's yours and mine
Always was, always is, always will be.

Paul Denegri- Music Volunteer at GCH

Lyrics from a Love Song

When We Nurse We Care

To Nurse and care for others
it's a blessing
In life it's not things,
it's the people,
they share their memories,
photos of family and friends,
their feelings,
smiles
laughter.

Life can be hard
and for some confusing,
hopefully we make life easier
peaceful for them,
and sometimes until they pass
especially when they have no family.
We do what some can't,
in a way no one else can.

Nina, ex Marie Curie nurse

Our Home

The Cyder Barn is a wonderful, comfy and charming place,
Where residents are treated with care, respect and grace.
There are scenic, countryside views including magical Glastonbury Tor,
And a pretty garden where we plant flowers, grow vegetables, herbs and more.
Daily exercises keep us fit, active and improve our well-being, so they say
Ending leg exercises with the "Can Can" brightens many a day.
We love to do daily activities and word games to keep us stimulated,

And if we happen to nod off, we do not get berated.
Sharing stories, photos and memories can be truly treasuring,
Age, race, religion, ability is not for measuring.
Sometimes we like to draw, paint and do craft,

Even creating silly hats no matter how simplistic and making us look daft.

Sundays we relish morning prayers and hymn singing,
Thankful and appreciative for everything we have, god willing.
Pub nights are a whizz, playing cards, darts, skittles and a quiz,
Enjoying a tasty finger buffet and a few bottles of fizz.
Monthly musical entertainers are full of fun,

With clapping, pom poms, laughter and popular songs sung.

Our handyman is brilliant at multi-tasking,
And sometimes fixes things without us asking.

Our hairdresser gives a good wash, trim and dry – keen to make us look our best,
She loves a good natter and helps us unwind and not feel stressed.
Perfect Piggies keep our toes and nails healthy and trim,
Our visiting dentist ensures our teeth match our grin.
The optician regularly tests our vision and our sight,
But some of his equipment may give you a fright.

The district nurse is a bubbly lass,
Who gives us medicine on a spoon or in a glass.
She's very gentle when she gives an injection
This is vital to prevent infection.

Our jolly chef produces delicious and nutritious food,
Together with his kitchen team, who are often in jovial mood.
The housekeepers are amazing for keeping our rooms tidy and clean,
Always making time to chat and glad we've overcome COVID-19.
Our carers are a compassionate, skilled and caring team,

Making our home a living dream.
Admin/Reception is a vital role,
The first point of contact to greet and enrol.

Our manager is a fantastic peer, who advises everyone sensibly and clear,
She's devoted to her residents and staff with plenty of cheer,

Also a much loved and respected dear.
All in all, we are friendly folk

Often enjoying a game, song, laugh and joke.
Growing old together and making new friends is not a worry,
Enjoying a slower pace of life and never in a hurry.
On the wall we display our family tree of which we are proud,

Visitors are welcome and always allowed.

By Activity Staff in collaboration with the residents.
The Cyder Barn Care Home

Our Home

The Snowflake

A white goddess drifted into the fire.
Only a gentle zephyr saw
Her journey into hell
With no mourning for lost beauty,
No tolling far away,
Quietly into nothing passed
A snowflake.

Donald Denegri
RIP 2021 Passed peacefully in a care home

I'm Telling Your Father

You wait until your Father gets home
It wasn't me what told Lizzie she could fly
As she jumped out of the tree
It was our Christopher not me
Don't tell fibs or it's bed for you
Without any tea
But it was not me
It was our Christopher
And him that put that toad in Grandma's tea
So he can go to bed without any tea
Not me
And he said he was the champion at conkers
But it's not him
It's me
Oh I can't wait till Father gets home..he he
I'm going out to play
Because it was him
Not me.

Jo Taylor
Housekeeper GCH

The Brook

The Brook

It's a wonderful sight to stand and look
at the slow moving water of the silent brook.
The gentle ripples in the water so clear
means the fish are swimming quite near.
Stepping stones placed where the river is wide
to enable ones cross to the other side.
Branches hang low from the swaying trees
and sweeps the water with their shining leaves.
Birds swoop down and duck their head,
to bite at fish on the river bed
and as day ends and night will fall
but in my mind I still recall,
what a wonderful sight to stand and look
at the slow moving water of the silent brook.

Written for Sally Knauer in 1973 by Joan Murphy

Let's Get Rocked

There is nothing like a rock gig.

Power
Headlong
These Are The Days of Our Lives
Here I Go Again
It's My Life
I Want To Break Free
.... so Pour Some Sugar on Me

..no longer a.. Slave to the Grind
..no longer on.. Dangerous Ground
..I'm on my.. Runaway Train
A Soldier of Fortune
..like it was.. The Summer of '69
Don't Stop Me Now
..because again I'm.. Wild Young and Free
Let Me Live
... and ... I'll Surrender
It's Rock or Bust
.... and.. All Night Long

Like A Hurricane
... I'm ... Thunderstruck
Hysteria
Adrenalize
Nothing Else Matters
I Want It All
... in.. A Decadance Dance
Do Anything You Want To Do
....but always... Jump
It's Harder to Breathe
Out of Control
It's Not Enough
...this.. Sweet Child of Mine
It's F.I.N.E
Everything Changes
In My Rock of Ages
So Let the Good Times Rock

..always remember.. God Gave Rock and Roll To You
....through our... Crazy Nights
..even when.. Love Bites
Cryin'
Crazy
Amazin'
You Shook Me All Night Long

And at ......

The Final Countdown
We All Die Young
In The Still of the Night
Back in Black
...the day will come when I... Close My Eyes Forever
..be.. Six Feet Under
On the Highway to Hell?
...no I'll... Shout At The Devil
.... I'm like a.. Fallen Angel
In The November Rain
Knockin' on Heavens Door
..giving me.. Something to Believe In

So there I'll stand at the gates ... Living On A Prayer
..and my body now ... Wasted Away
Send Me An Angel
.. please, please, remember I.... Once Had A Heart
...and my life was ... Home Sweet Home

...to you all I'll ... See You On The Other Side
...but...Don't Go Away Mad Go Away Even
Have A Little Faith
..and... Two Steps Behind You
The Gangs All Here
For Those About To Rock We Salute You
The Best Is Yet To Come

I Remember You

By Jon Bon Jovi's Boots

Overboard

It feels as if this morning's storm
Has carried the world's suffering
To this place.

The sky opens,
And lost souls shinny down
Slivers of rain.

Or jump from leaves
- Impossibly high -
To shatter on the ground.

From where they come,
I do not know.
Their tales I can only guess.

Strangely, I find solace in the fruit,
On the forest floor.
Acorn, chestnut, and sycamore.

Seeds of renewal,
From which a wood will rise,
And its canopy embrace us all.

Simon Denegri OBE

Autumn Wind

Here I am entering,
I can feel your breath on my skin,
my hairs stand on ends,
can hear you whispering, to your friends.

Feeling like there's eyes on me,
I know you're watching me,
when I look, everything is still,
suddenly feel the chill.

Is this for real? or all in my head,
there's flowers in bed,
the birds fly, high in the sky,
as trees sway from side to side,

like they're dancing in the wind,
the angelic voice that you sing,
the sky darkens, nights are drawing in,
fall is coming, leaves are falling,

I'm overwhelmed with emotion,
colours of orange and brown explosion,
I can feel you closing in,
my god,
the Autumn wind

Samuel Gwilliam
Mum worked in care

Rainbow Scarves

Pastel shades of rainbow colour
Arch itself around the sun
Hugging it like a silk scarf would,
Colours that appeared
When the raindrops began.
Birds singing whilst preparing their nest
And, for just a moment
They stop to welcome the cool
Shower in the midst of of hot sun,
But there's no time to rest.

Picnics by the river
Couples young and in love,
Dragonflies mirror metallic reflections
Along the water's edge,
Whilst butterflies with velvet wings
Dance through the air without a care.

Children lay in the grass and
Make pictures from the candy floss clouds
Oh yes it's true
Castles in the sky really do exist,
With rainbow waterfalls,
Red, yellow, pink and green
Pastel shades of a rainbow scarf
Brings a smile to my face
As I sit in my field of daisies,
How beautiful is the view
As I watch the world
Float hazily on by.

Sam Kilburn
Senior Carer GCH

Rainbow Scarves
Illustration by Sam Kilburn

Under The Old Willow Tree

Under the moon's gaze
An old willow tree sways,
Whilst a soft breeze of a cool wind
Silently blows and through it's branches
I am sure
I can almost hear it whispering your name

From beneath the old willow tree,
As I look high above captivated
By the moon as it lights up the night sky
Reflecting in the dark river below.
Stars twinkling casting their rays
Both near and far
I smile and take a deep breath
Wiping away a tear
I can feel you near,
Your arms wrapped around me
In a warm embrace

I shut my eyes
And make a wish,
I wish that you find love
And are also loved,
And that you are always happy
And safe from harm

From my heart that stands alone
Under the old willow tree,
Via a kiss blown on the breeze
Of a silent wind,
My wish is now yours
As I do send it to thee
And as it brushes past your lips
You'll hear me whisper your name.

Sam Kilburn
Senior Carer GCH

My Day

Alarm! Wake up but not awake.
I ache
From head to toe
From elbow to elbow
Do 'me' in these first few minutes
And then attend to everyone else
Who assumes I have no limits
The true me is soon done
Now my work face has begun

Get in car
Don't feel like a star
Before I turn the key
Who is the real me?
Can I keep going again
Sing, drive, emotionally drain
Drive in

Where it will all begin.
Walk through the door
What greets me is the same and more
Walk into room after room
Smile but have to remember no gloom!

Whatever I feel
It's not their deal
'Hi how are you this morning?'
Daft question all things considering
I say it nonetheless
It's an automatic process
I don't have a heart of steel
I quickly feel
This isn't just a job
And I'm not a snob

They rely on me
Not to feel crappie
With priceless minutes of life left
How can I think to be bereft?
I've cared all day, but not for me
How can this be?
I feel and look a mess
Hardened face through the stress

Since daylight I've given all to all
Juggling many a ball
Tried not to drop one
Means life and death all said and done
Told by those that advise
Who say they are wise.
Put the gas mask on you first right?
Then you care for others' plight
Thing is
And this is the biz
I can't think where my gas mask is
It's just another task, a big ask
What don't they understand?
It's out of my hands
My heart is care
I want to share
It's my destiny, my roadway
Home to give even more
This time to those closer whom I adore
My patience is limited now
It's hard not to scowl

Finally bed and light out
Think lots of doubt
Finally alone in my space
This moment I must embrace
But I ache
Head to toe
From elbow to elbow
I nod off fast
Another day of life has passed
I sleep and deep
Until that bloody alarm goes beep!

Shirley, Nurse

New Admission

Word starts to go around
from the ground up, anticipation builds
The excitement slowly mounts
And only one question hangs in the air,
Is it a male?
Is it a female?
The room is ready
Bed-rails are down
Staff are eager
ready to deliver
But the question still remains,
Is it a male?
Is it a female?
Tradition dictates the question be asked
But gender matters not
Either male or female
The care remains the same
And only one thing is for certain
It's a new admission.

William Muchochomi
Carer GCH

I no longer dare to care

I no longer dare to care,
My heart I've tucked away
Deep within my soul
There at least,
I know all of its pieces are safe
Locked away, buried
With my memories that
No one can take

I no longer dare to care to speak
For my word is never heard
And I'll never get the answers I seek
My eyes have seen too much pain
The truth of life has left me
Feeling drained

I no longer dare to care
Too many times
I've been knocked to the ground
Too many times
I got up and tried
No more, I can't,
I won't not this time
I'll stay here with my head
In my hands
I'll not have hope
Or faith in fate (Cont)

It can go and find someone else
For I can't pretend
And live this life you've made

No longer willing to let you
See how much it hurts
I won't cry as I look you in your eyes
And finally you'll hear the words
I've dared never to say
"Goodbye now it is your turn to cry"

And as the pain grows
And my silent tears flow,
Growing older with each day passing,
I begin to understand now
With my broken heart
I was never destined to be a whole
I would rather no longer dare to care
Than to learn what it feels like to hate,
As I say my final goodbye.

Sam Kilburn
Senior Carer GCH

No Longer Dare to Care
Illustration by Sam Kilburn

I'm Tired

I'm tired of this rage,
Stuck in this cage,
Trying to be someone I'm not.
I'm not your golden child.
I'm not your model of a child.
How can I learn when you shout at me:
Don't talk; answer every question.
Stay still; run fast; try harder.
Walk on the lines - nice and straight,
Single file; don't be late.
I'm tired of this charade
I'm tired of being your parade
Pranced around like a trophy.
Outstanding, is apparently what "we" are if we:
Don't talk; answer every question.
Stay still; run fast; try harder.
Walk on the lines - nice and straight,
Single file; don't be late.
Stay in the box, don't flap your hands
Memorise every text known to man.
But YOU can't do one thing for ME.
You deny my EHCP whilst I:
Don't talk; answer every question.
Stay still; run fast; try harder.
Walk on the lines - nice and straight,

Single file; don't be late.
You mould us, you scold us,
Then tell us to be kind.
We can't ever speak what's on our mind.
The counsellor's waiting list is months away
And I'm tired.
But who cares? As long as I
Don't talk; answer every question.
Stay still; run fast; try harder.
Walk on the lines - nice and straight,
Repress all my emotion and don't be late.
I'm rewarded as I
Hide myself; sit up straight;
Wear my uniform and get good grades.
Top button up; even if I can't breathe,
You don't see the scratches beneath my sleeves.
I'm tired of this rage,
Stuck in this cage,
Trying to be someone I'm not.
I'm not your golden child.
I'm not your model of a child.
How can I learn when you shout at me:
Don't talk; answer every question.
Stay still; run fast; try harder.
Walk on the lines - nice and straight,
Single file; don't be late.

By Harriet Lewis - This poem was written and performed by Harriet at a S.E.N.D reform protest this year in Norwich

Remembering You

I may not remember you as others do.
By entries past in monogrammed diaries,
Or symbols, marks and numbers scored,
On the calendar hanging behind the kitchen door.

I may not remember you as I should, some might say.
With framed photographs, or disciplined candles,
Well-worn toasts over warming wine,
Or the recalling of your name time after time.

No, it is in the aching passage of the day –
The extra place setting foolishly laid, and the waiting bed,
With white sheets tucked and made –
That I will remember you.

Ordinary days
You made extraordinary.
Now emptied and made solitary.

But time will pass and it will be you that remembers me.
In the sun's rays falling on my shoulders
Or the rain tapping at my window.

You will find me
And your memory will warm me
In the harshest climes.

I am sure of that
For we love each other like no others can.

Simon Denegri OBE

Remembering You

Dawn

The moon its modest nightwatch done
With dignity fades away
As the strident sun awakens the day
All nature is aroused from sleep
Prepared its responsibility to keep:
The flora to fulfill its promise to bloom
The birds to sing and nest
The handsome trees to look their foliage best
And the valleys and hills to flourish
For what more could we wish?

Donald Denegri
RIP 2021 Passed peacefully in a care home

Dawn

Thanks from a student nurse

I arrived on the ward as green as grass,
Early in the morning my eyes glazed like glass,
So much to learn, so much to do, excuse me,
What's that? A Lapy who?

It isn't easy when you haven't a clue
Waiting for the next experienced cue.
But you all made me feel welcome
And taught me a lot
And made me feel less of a clumsy clot!

I did temps, and pulses (I thought those were beans)
Now the mud's cleared
I know what these terms mean!
Making ward beds is quite an art,
How to tuck corners so they look smart.
Catheters, drains and drips
All in a day's shift

From afar a little voice asks
"Can you help us to lift?"
"Which end do I grip,
The patient or the drip?"
The patients face gets grayer and grayer
As they look at this uniformed
'L' plate slayer!

With your ceaseless patience,
Kindness and care
I have reached another goal
Hurrah I'm there
I've learned so much my knowledge increased
I'm now going to leave you in peace.
Thank you all so much,
I've enjoyed my stay,
My time has finished I must away.

Love and thanks Amelia x

By RMN Amelia, GCH, on first student placement at Yeovil Hospital

Alone in Rio

If you were here,
Sugarloaf Mountain would be
All the sweeter.
And 'Christ the Redeemer'
Could relax his arms.
We could make love in the heat,
Then sleep.
Instead I sweat out old battles under
The sheet.

If you were here,
The air conditioning would not blow
Hot and cold.
We would have been upgraded to First,
And we would have ventured
Beyond the hotel,
To quench our thirst.

Yes, if you were here,
We would be drinking this
city together.
From a bar overlooking
Copacabana.
In wide screen format,
In technicolour.
Making up words
To 'The Girl from Ipanema.'

But instead, you are half-way round the world,
And I am sharing photos of places
I half-heartedly been
Half-seen.
If only you were here.

Simon Denegri OBE

The Devil

The Devil he comes among us
Time and time again
He tries to tear our world apart
And loves to see our pain
But we are strong, we seldom weep
We stand and show our pride
Ladies, men and children
Standing side by side
The marvel of the people and the
Wondrous things they do
To heal and feed and help us
Just pray we'll all come through
Don't listen to the moaners and
The stories that they tell
Introduce them to the Devil
And tell them go to hell.

Joan Murphy - written during the first Covid lock down.

Remember Me

Remember me for the good times
But for the stormy times too,
That we weathered together
And came out stronger
Than we could have foreseen
Also for the ordinary times
That left no trace
Except we were together
And were cradled in that special pleasure
That is mutual family love.

Do not grieve for me
I take my special memories with me
And in whatever light or darkness is my lot
I will nourish my soul with them
And bless you for the special love
That bound us together.

Donald Denegri
RIP 2021 passed peacefully in a care home

I See You

COMMUNITY SOCIAL FUND

Recording day for the I See You Song 2022

The I See You Fund was formed as a response to a vision by Paul Denegri a local professional musician and music volunteer at Glastonbury Care Home who wants to inspire, encourage and support professional, amateur and young musicians to bring live music into care homes across the UK, to help those in the last years of their lives find enjoyment and peace of mind

Paul wrote, produced, performed and released a single called I See You at the end of 2022 which GCH tied in with the launch of the I See You Social Community Fund. It is an extremely moving and powerful song with an accompanying video filmed inside the care home to help raise awareness of the dedicated care that is happening in care homes 24/7 all over the world.

We are so grateful to Paul for his creativity, skills, passion and funding towards such a wonderful initiative. Since the release of the single last Christmas Paul and GCH have continued to raise funds for this very important cause.

If you would like to apply to the fund on behalf of anyone who resides in care and is in need of financial assistance please email the home: glastonbury@brunelcare.org.uk

Scan the QR code if you would like to hear the song , or copy the link onto your browser

https://youtu.be/2ryTliCaEeg

Jo Taylor performing her poem to residents at GCH

If you would like to donate please search Glastonbury Care Home on Just Giving or via bank transfer details below:
Sort code: 60 : 17 : 12
Account Number 66909473
Using reference CN04 ISY

"I See You looks such a good idea and importantly in an area that people outside of the care sector are unaware of. Sadly all too often the ones I come across are lonely or lack the simple basics of life through no fault of their own but it is these small things rather than big gestures that make such a difference. Wishing you well in your wonderful efforts " - **Shirley (Nurse)**

"Good work guys. Keep it up and thanks for your dedication" - **Mark and Jan Curtis Just Giving**

"So important we look after the elderly please please keep going raising money and awareness" - **Anon, Just Giving**

"Please keep doing all you can in raising awareness" - **Just Giving**

Other titles published by Pandon also available on Amazon

*A Poem for Every Day
by Donald Denegri*

*Two on the Shore and
other Short Stories by
Donald Denegri*

*Simple Prayers for
Simple Needs by
Donald Denegri*

https://www.justgiving.com/fundraising/glastonbury-care-home

Printed in Great Britain
by Amazon